Fair's Fair

Susan Utting was born in South London and brought up against a shifting background of pubs, cafés and ballroom dancing. She studied Creative Writing at the University of Sussex, after graduating in English, Film and Drama at Reading University where she worked for many years, first in the Psychology Department and then as Poetry and Creative Writing tutor. Awards include The Peterloo Poetry Prize, an Arts Council Laureateship, The Berkshire Poetry Prize, an Academi Cardiff prize and Poetry Business prize for *Something Small is Missing* (Smith/Doorstop). Her work was selected for *The Times* newspaper's 'Best Love Poem' feature, has appeared in *The Times Literary Supplement*, *The Independent* and *The Forward Book of Poetry*. Following *Striptease* (Smith/Doorstop, 2001) and *Houses Without Walls* (Two Rivers Press, 2006), *Fair's Fair* is Susan Utting's third full collection of poetry.

Fair's Fair

Susan Utting

For Tom,

Best wishes

Susan Utting

Albion Beatnik, OXFORD
2016

TWO
RIVERS
PRESS

First published in the UK in 2012 by Two Rivers Press
7 Denmark Road, Reading RG1 5PA.
www.tworiverspress.com

ISBN 978-1-901677-80-5

2 3 4 5 6 7 8 9

Two Rivers Press is represented in the UK by Inpress Ltd and
distributed by Central Books.

Cover design and illustration by Sally Castle.
Text design by Nadja Guggi and typeset in Janson and Parisine.

Printed and bound in Great Britain by Imprint Digital, Exeter.

*In memory of my parents,
Sue and Ron of the Blue Ball Inn*

Acknowledgements

Thanks are due to the editors of the following publications
where some of these poems first appeared:

Times Literary Supplement
The North (45)
Ink Sweat & Tears
Kaleidoscope (Cinnamon Press)
Reading Poetry (Two Rivers Press)
Spring (Gatehouse Press)
Paper Planes (University of Reading Creative Arts)
Taking the Biscuit (URCA)
Insert Your Life Story Here (URCA)
Nothing Like Concrete (URCA)

'Under the Blue Ball' won the Peterloo Poetry Prize 2007.
'Dictation' was shortlisted for the Bridport Prize 2011.

I am grateful to Tŷ Newydd and The Taliesin Trust;
to Adrian Blamires and Allison McVety for their insightful
comments and suggestions; and to Carol Ann Duffy,
Gillian Clarke and Penelope Shuttle for their inspiration
and encouragement.

Contents

III.

Foreword

Across the open pages of the book
poems come in two by two, like
creatures coupled in a strange ark.

I.

Of pleasures, the unsurreptitious.
Of aims, the adventitious.
—Bertolt Brecht, from *Orge's List of Wishes*

Giving Up Mirrors

Like giving up the time (take off your watch,
unplug the glowing digits, let the chiming clock
run down to silent) there will be things
that catch you out.
                        The whole world turns
to glass and chrome, plays tricks with darkened
screens, with windows day and night, with water.
You will be tempted.
                          Be prepared to stick at it.
Stay indoors, keep shutters shut, curtains drawn,
if there's a glint, sew up the edges.

When all the looking glasses face their walls,
the last fixed mirror's sheeted over, wait.
Sit still. Let dust gather, soften the focus.
One day at a time
                      you'll learn to look out
through eyes that have forgotten old reflected
selves, that see the world for all it is, and wonder
at its unexamined shine.

Thetis

They call me *shape-shifter*, as if my skill
were sin: true self's a myth as much
as *wysiwyg* tripped off glib tongues,
the empty vessel's rattle. I am a bowl

that fills itself with luscious fruits,
the beady loveliness of shucked peas
or at a whim may bubble to its brim
with pale, delicious wine. At will

I'll burnish to a brassy glow,
take on the lustre of bone china,
or tire of a fine finish and turn rough
as a rustic thumb-pot. My gist

is mutable, a feast wherein I choose
each delectation, each incarnate moment.

Naked

More than I'd seen before, more
than a rabbit, skinned by the sleight
of a butcher's hands, much more than

the deft red of his wrists. More than
a plucked bird on a hook like a capital
ess in a copperplate book and more

than a grandmother's mouth stripped
of its keyboard, its click and grin, more
than the gloss of her chopperless gums.

More than his startled skin, its gooseflesh
and quiver, the gristle that made him *boy*,
more than his ears without their pink wires,

more than all that, lacking their circles
of glass, the blur and fuzz of their squint
looking back at me, more naked than Adam
after the apple: the boy in the bathroom's eyes.

Girl at the Window

after Oskar Kokoschka

Inside, the bird in its cage swings
on its swing, small as a wren but black
as a rook, no tongue in its head to sing,
no glint in its eye for the weather.

Outside there's a full moon touched
by clouds and the stars are out like
Christmas; trees droop with the weight
of their leaves, and still no rain has fallen.

The girl leans on the sill, half out,
half in, the book on her lap lies open,
her face is pale as a winter moon,
her hands crossed neat as wings.

She tilts on her stool, stares out,
the words in her head unspoken;
small as a wren, black as a rook,
the bird in its cage swings on.

Wanting the Moon

If I could choose
Freely in that great treasure-house
Anything from any shelf,
I would give you back yourself ...
—Edward Thomas

The sky is as wide as a sleepless night
and I miss the moon. I want it out,
the whole of its fat face, flat
as a tin badge with a lopsided smile.

Like a child who climbs on a roof,
clings to the stack of the chimney
and weeps till her tears loosen the mortar,
unsteady the bricks, turn soot to a salt-water
trickle that drip, drips on the stubborn hearth,
I want the moon.

                I want it to sweep your face
bright as a searchlight, to find you, head tilted,
chin up, lips making words at the ink of the sky;
I want the moon to know what it is you are saying.

Learning to Read

She remembered her first time, top deck of the bus,
a spiral of stripes on a pole, and *Barber's Shop*
see-sawed itself to her tongue, came out as a sing-
song of *baa baa sheep*, close but a fumble. Then
clap hands, she got it! Soon they were everywhere,
easy as peasy, shapes for the taking, into her head,
out through her mouth in oceans of hisses, lisps,
clackings, mooings, flibbertigibbets of mouth-music.

Everywhere now, till she couldn't forget, till delight,
without clapping its hands, without moving its lips,
turned itself weary, to a tune in her head she couldn't
switch off, a gushing tap stuck at full on. How she
narrowed her eyes at the *Bus Stop*, at *Lyons Maid*,
Little Horse Close, tried to get back to the patterns
as patterns, squinnying hard to unfocus, to skim over
Stop! Children Crossing! Last Day of Sale, over *Entrance*,
No Ball Games, This Door is Alarmed and *No Exit*.

The Line

Our feet are small enough to slip inside
each other's shoes, we're stitched together
at the heels by a long thread, clever
as the run-and-fell of a blind hem.

Our bodies grew together once, mine
bulged with her, the thread between us
then was fat with blood. A kite string
cuts the palm of my hand, I don't know

how to steer or guide it; all I can do
is keep on playing out the line, make
circles in the air, unwind my hand, look up
and watch its wind-tugged, lovely flight.

Drinking with Sarah

Her laugh's like brandy, its amber, copper glow,
the way it clings to the sides of glass balloons,
that sweet, slow trickle.
                    What do we know of brandy,
she and I – we don't rub narrow shoulders with hard
drinkers, lush tipplers, after-dinner connoisseurs
who, full and mellow, cup their palms around cut glass
to spin thin gold, who dip their noses to inhale.

We sip coffee, tea from thick-walled mugs, steam-heat
our cheeks and squint our eyes for pleasure, keep
our faces straight for non-sequential links, their logic.
What matters is inconsequential talk, how lives out loud
turn tragedy ridiculous.
                    What do I know of this, except
that Sarah laughs and it is brandy-wine, its slow, belly-
warming swirl, its afterglow.

Over

And everything fell together, repeated itself
like an old-fashioned pattern, like moss stitch,
stocking, cable, rib; we widened our eyes
at the over-and-over, the cruel way that it was.

Like wool-hoarders, hedging our stocks
for austerity's bite, the ration of lean years
that follows a war, we began to unpick,
outstretching our arms for the dip and
wind of unravelling yarn, over our fingers,
under our palms, into a thickening ball.

Over and over we'd slip out our fingers,
start winding again, adjusting the slant
to keep the shape even, symmetric,
round; aesthetic as motherhood.

Picture of my Mother as a Young Woman

Look at her flirt in her flash-vivid bolero,
lash-flutter, hair-flick and kiss-me-soft smile:
she's wearing the sequins and satin, gold thread
embroidery, pleated-sleeved, edge-to-edge moiré
coatee, that was bargained-for, haggled and smuggled,
swaddled in khaki, shouldered by kitbag through
mud-field and cart-track, held river-high, ocean-dry,
sky-dropped and army-truck-juddered away from
the home-fire promisers, gunfire & bonhomie.
        Look at her, girlish as romance, done up
to kill in the glitter-bright bolero, sweet-hearted,
rescued and true as a love-token, trophy or spoil.

Distances

From the glint in the eye
to the one-eyed stare,

from the clack of high heels
to the high-backed chair,

from the hot black and strong
to the sugared full cream,

to the spoon fed soup
from the china tureen.

To the winceyette nap
from the black watered silk,

to nothing to say
from nothing but talk,

to *under the weather*
from *over the moon*,

from the cocktail umbrella
to this darkened room.

Fair's Fair

We are not all able to do all things
—Virgil, *Eclogues* viii

Lend me your quickstep twinkle, your Highland Schottische
and I'll lend you the flex of my knees, my steady toes, my hop
for your shuffle, your ballet fingers for my bitten thumbs.

For your stockpot skim, take the taste on my tongue – it's
all yours – and I'll give you a go with the bite of my teeth,
my jaws for your chomp on a liquorice log and a whole tray

of nut brittle – I'll give you the hammer, throw in the brass dog
for the walnuts. If you lend me your marzipan basket of flowers,
the weave and flow of your piping-bag nozzle, your spatula's lick

and the last scrape of your caterer's bowl, I'll bring you an unshaken
bottle of Jersey gold-top and a stiff drink in a straight glass, pink
elephant ice for a triple, nudged out from the blind eye of the optic.

Lend me your strong crop, its pepper-and-salt, and I'll lend you
my pump-water mouse, my pale cheek for your cock-a-snook. Give me
your tall larder of tales, the false and the true and the half-way there:

I'll give them the cut of my jib, my threading eye for your invisible darn.

The Things

For want of a foot, the shoe wept
like a babe in the crook of the wrong
woman's arm, it wouldn't be cradled
but struggled, arched itself, threw back
its tongue, dug in its heel, would not
be swayed, lullabied, softened.

For want of a fist, the glove snivelled,
skinnied itself to a pale thing, a shadow
of thumb, fore, thimble, ring, little,
to skin without bone, papery hide without
flesh. For want of a body the frocks sulked,
shouldered their hangers resentful as sinners

kept in, grounded away from the glitterball;
for want of a generous hip, for a bosom
to swathe, for a soft crease to reveal,
for a valley, a silk-stockinged thigh to flash
through their slashes, an ankle or calf
to show off their kick pleats, for want

of a woman with meat on her bones
they frayed, threadbared, tarnished,
rusted themselves to an obsolete regiment.
For want of some rhythm, muscle,
blood, for want of a voice, the things
stilled themselves, quietened; fell apart.

Warhol Blonde

What you don't remember is the way
she fades to smudge, to mono-
chrome, to feint, to whiteout.

You don't forget the yellow hair,
the slash of a carmine mouth,
that charcoal edge, the turquoise

lids that match the wings
of a stand-up collar; or the clash
of tangerine behind the linctus

pink of skin. There she is,
twice five times five, all half-
closed eyes and kiss-me pout,

a set of flick-book movie stills,
again, again and over, nothing
changing but the colours.

What shocks you now is not
acrylic zing or canvas weave,
the irony of mock-naive repeat,

it's what you see you had
forgotten: all that shadow,
its hide and seek, its chill.

Lament for Susie Green

No more the wicked tongue, the lizard skin shoes,
the cerise and black, no more the oyster and blue;

no more the filthy look, the thrupenny bits, no silver
or bronze, no more sixpence-suspenders, no lash-glitter.

No more the cochineal bottle, no bitters, no sauce, no
salt-pinch, no ice-chink, no backchat and no maraschino;

no more the pussyfoot kick, no more swift ones, no halves,
no more two fingers, no specials or jugs, no straight glasses.

No red hat, no fur coat, no Chantilly lace, no pins in the mouth,
no grosgrain or petersham, frogging or darting, no snowing-down-south.

No more the dog-see-the-rabbit, no go joe, no rabbit, no cricket, no score,
no peplum or jabot, gadget or slingback, no hip-shimmy heel spin; no more.

Cold Dark Matter: *An Exploded View*

after Cornelia Parker

If wood and metal danced they'd jig, like this:
a hokey-cokey whoop, into the middle and out,
into the middle and out in a bow and scrape
of splinter and scrap;
                iron, timber, rafter, plank,
                hinge, jamb, architrave, purlin,
circassian circle of jiggle and weave, they would
hoe-down the notion of *floor, ceiling, window, door;*
unstitched from their shadows they'd let themselves
go willy-nilly, a hop-skip and sashay, a dosey-doh
        knees-up, a that's-what-it's-all-about giggle.

Under the Blue Ball

Here's where the glittering queen bee descends
every night, with a creak from the rickety spiral,
ducks under the lintel where strangers' heads crack.

Here's where curmudgeons guard seats by the fire,
the inglenook regulars tapping their pipes out
where roll-ups and full strength have kippered the walls,

where bluebottles buzz in with stable lads steaming
like horses; where bets are laid, arrows thud, dominoes clatter
and cribbage gets rowdy with *one-for-his-nob* of a Friday.

When the bitter gets lively a knife skims the froth, the mild's
dark and dangerous, tasty as treacle, the Stingo's a kick to it,
Barley Wine's kept out the back for the brave or the foolish.

At last orders the landlady holds up the ceiling, wedges the door back
to let out the fug, and over the road the dead shake their headstones
to Country & Western played on the jukebox, or Victor Silvester

slipped in by the landlord. While invisible feet tread the boards
overhead, the hands of the long-dead lift latches at midnight
to join in the lock-in with hippies and huntsmen, jowl by cheeking

with blind-eyed law officers, majors and grease monkeys,
chippies and smallholders. Butcher and cheese-maker, flagstone
and fag ash, here's the whole world under rafter and roof-thatch.

Stickler

After all these years, there you are at the door
with your usual grin, like you've just popped in
for a chat, for a chew of the fat or some trouble
that strikes you as funny. It's not that I'm not really

glad you are back, with your shock of white thatch –
snow on the roof, fire in the hearth – your corduroy
forehead, unruly eyebrows, the long lobes of your ears.
And it's not that I don't feel more safe in a world with you

back with a swing of your capable arms, a rub of your thumbs
with their neat squared-off nails – I have missed your guffaws
and baritone roars, your unalloyed joy at the fact of my being
just me and all yours. It's just that I signed all the papers, swore

you were gone, invited the guests to your wake, threw in
a handful of soil. I auctioned your table (it made a good price),
gave back your regalia, medals and whatnot, I passed on
the watchmaker's loop, the sea-captain's whistle, your weatherglass.

So it feels like a blasphemy, heresy, illegal act – like a lie, and you,
a stickler for straight talk and truth, you wouldn't rest easy with that.

II.

Of abodes, the impermanent.
Of partings, the unexuberant.
—Bertolt Brecht, from *Orge's List of Wishes*

You

When I came in that night, that almost
day, you were a ghost: a grown woman,
tall, moon-faced, crazy-eyed, the usual
white and grey. Your feet had gone,

or hid themselves – you drifted, moved
your mouth, shaped your lips to words;
none came, not even breath. We stood
eye to eye, stared. Time passed.

I shifted, breathed. Closer, I saw you
flimsy as gauze, an ectoplasmic trick –
I walked right through you.

Cock crow, sound of a bird,
first light, and you, long gone.

Not You

I want to show you the ragged vine
that's climbed the branch that hangs
itself across the fence, the weed that's
tipped the apple tree with foreign
blossoms in November; to tell you

that it's there, these mornings when
I look out, check the flicker of leaves,
their shiver, spin and fall. I want you
to wait with me, watch for the trees
to bare themselves to crooked bones,

to see it all through slatted blinds –
the tips and roofs, the spire that hid
all Summer; to know they've been
there all along, obdurate, intact.

Dreamer

When the body sleeps, at first it turns
anti-clockwise, winds itself in search of some sweet
swaddled infancy where sleep comes rocked and lulled
by chanted spells, by *Jeannie with the light brown hair*,
the smiling *angels up above you*, the husky whisperings
of weary motherers.

The sleeping body grows,
turns its tricks, ages, becomes that strange country
where cliff-edge fallers hang in the air, where even
journeys along straight, familiar roads don't end in *home*;
where lines once known by heart stay on the edge
of the mind's eye, the tip of the idle tongue.

And while it frets
and spins through all those restless tropes and lullabies,
as it takes on the marks of its own weight – a creased
cheek, an etched forearm, the scars of another life –
the sleeping body turns itself again clockwise,
searching for its rescuer, its clear-eyed, waking self.

Dictation

It is the after-lunch, the p.m. dip, the bellyful of
three more hours to go against the bodyclock
that wants to slow itself, to droop its lids, to drift.

And she's not listening to a word he says, she's
hearing him in light and shade, in curves and dashes,
a tick, a hook, the beautiful economy of short-forms.

She's ahead of him, more words per minute than his
voice can rattle while she dozes and her pencil runs
the page on tiptoe, hushing with its *light and lighter still.*

She's on automatic, sleepy mistress of the air, translating
waves to codes that he cannot decipher – she hasn't listened
to a word and still she has it all verbatim; sound for sound

she reads him back, astonished at the words her own
voice makes, at what he's told, at what she's telling him.

Hong Kong Side

The lift hums, tells us this is *Monday*.
We are cool, too cool, the air is artificial,
noisy. Then we're out and heat slaps
our faces – you're ready for it, I am thin,
pale, English, thirsty for drizzle, dizzy, faint.

I try to breathe, try not to breathe in rot
of fish, flesh, dead meat, piss, dog, human
ordure. This is before Lan Tau, the temple,
the climb, the stumble, the split.
                                        This
is Hong Kong Side, still sleazy-rich,
before rebellion, lying down, taking it.

Now

Amsterdam without
you, or you, or even you:

this time it's easy,
lazy, beautiful, as strong

as coffee, fresh as
red shutters on high windows,

friendly as geraniums
on winking canal water.

Altering the Clocks

This is not the time for falling back
to thoughts of the dying of bees,
of fathers, sisters, daughters, held
by a steady thread of prayer, mouthed
or hummed in the heads of unbelievers.

We have passed the danger days,
the anniversaries of the *one sure thing*
and reached the time to spring forward
into the light of afternoons, their growing
warm, to the tips of green things that will

push up through the mud, we know they will
unfurl themselves, like memories of the dead
they'll come again; at the altering of clocks
we reach the safe time, move closer to believers.

October

Each morning a fresh windfall to gather
and light growing precious, shifting
in time with the clocks.

                    Each leaf
from a neighbour's tree, from my own,
falls soft on the damp lawn, huddles itself
in a bunch with the wind, with its
yellowing, goldening kind.

Now there's a quickening chill in the air
that makes itself smoke, that will pinch
at my cheeks before long, redden
my fingers, bite tender shoots black,
turn leaves, gusted to heaps, to a shiver.

                    Here are promises, too:
the thrill that will come at the end of a year
turning itself to the *now* of a memory, warm
in the house of the heart, quick in the blood,
close as the touch of an old love.

Postcard Home

There's weather here, but so far no-one's
mentioned it. There are trees, too, and one,
they say, was once believed the tallest in the world.

Remember the mulberry? The uncut grass,
the glut that year we lived on cigarettes and bread,
cheap wine and bitter berries? Remember the juice?
And all those woody pips.
                              Our tree was fat
as a greenwood fairytale, and tall, the tallest
we could see from where we were.

From where I am it's a detail, a thumbnail, a faraway
word, three beats in a line from a children's rhyme,
a cold and frosty morning trick of the rhythm.

Most Easterly

I don't remember trees, just grass, flat dunes,
seaholly skeletons and the marks of hooves
in the sand like dust. I don't remember horses.

I remember Ernie's kayak, us (foolhardy, unfazed
by the chop and swirl of North Sea grey) dragging
the light-hulled thing like a bodkin through rough cloth,

over the rough-trod track and down to the slip and pull
at the smooth edge. I remember our scramble in,
(me unsteady, you *steady!*) the cold whip on our skin,

our bodies' tilt, the paddles' dip and lift. Steady
together: arms, blades, wings, the swoop of the gulls
behind, the coast as far out east as it gets, behind us

everything pulling us back, the stretch of the sea
ahead for as far as our salt-stung eyes could see.

Going Home

Home is not where I come from;
home is where I'm going.

Home slips from my lips without thought:
the fit of an odd number, the ring
of the name of a street, chosen
years ago now, known even then
without learning. There have been arms

like that, warm bodies, easy and close
as my own interlaced fingers.
This morning the sea is a stranger,
another's salt on my skin,
an unfamiliar address that disturbs

thought, that interrupts sleep
with its breathing. I'm moving away
from this noisy shore, inland, back
to the steady to-and-fro of myself,
back to brick, blossom, tarmac, bud,

click and shiver, skitter and creak,
to the comfort of sounds in the night
that I'll know like the sound of my
own heart in my ear, that I'll know
well enough not to hear, not to listen for.

Leaving

Three days and nights of snow had royal iced the lawn,
made fondant shapes of trees, muffled their footfalls.
They laboured all the fourth day afternoon with shovels,
garden spades and trowels, to build a family of snow:
a round robin of five in staggered heights.

Inside, they slapped and hugged themselves, shook
fingers back to life and rubbed each other's hands
and toes against the hot-aches. He told them
over mugs of soup, around the fire that kept on
with its spit and crackle while their chatter guttered.

After that they kept to their rooms, heads down
avoided talk, eye contact across landings. But she,
the youngest one, still saw October's sharp-toothed
grins, November's flame-lashed effigies; she saw
the coal-eyed stares of people made of snow.

The Weight of Snow

Once there was snowfall, settled
so deep it would bury a child, light
as a feather swung up on his shoulders,
her father's, an hour of his trudging
and still she was *nothing like heavy*.

Once there were snowball fights,
coal eyes and mufflers, heavy falls
that broke hip bones, fragile from
wartime, a snow queen who left
icy splinters of glass in a heart.

Once there was snow on a bride,
on her veil on the day, when April
was tricked into winter, too late for
the snowdrops, too soon for his roses,
just time for the flown-over lilies.

Now there's this: a bubble of glass,
a scene under water, pocket of air,
a chapel, people, the slip of a path
to a cottage, its whitening roof,
its story-book chimneystack;

feel its weight, cold sentimental,
its lie, smooth as a fairytale.

Before the Storm

The forecast is for thunder, rain,
air presses, iron bands my head –
I'm covering mirrors, hiding knives again.

The ritual is well-learned, a game
we played when crackled wireless voices said
the forecast was for thunder, rain.

Each day is heavy weather, I could blame
the atmospheric weight before the storm, instead
I'm covering mirrors, hiding knives again.

Quotidian's the same-old, same-old same,
no shocks, no claps or flashes though I've read
the forecast is for thunder. Rain

would be a blessing. It's not for shame
I have to swaddle glass, put blades to bed,
cover mirrors, hide the knives again,

I'm caught, a link between links in a chain
of superstitious women who have led
me, each time the forecast is for thunder, rain,
covering mirrors, hiding knives again.

III.

Of lives, the lucid.
Of deaths, the rapid.
—Bertolt Brecht, from *Orge's List of Wishes*

Everywhere

Everywhere, love surfaces, rises
from its bench and arm-in-arms it
along city streets, hangs out on corners,
joshing, fluttering, not quite canoodling.

Love blocks the escalators with its huddle,
at café tables, head to head, it stares at
fingertips that don't quite touch, to watch
the sparks that jump across the gap.

Spring is not the season, this is back-end
blustery and dull, no Indian Summer
daft reminder of what warmth just was;
yet heat is everywhere, shimmering

from bodies as they two-by-two it, pink-
cheeked, adolescent, ripening with love.

Love, Like Salt

"What shall Cordelia do? Love, and be silent."
—*King Lear*, Act I Sc. 1

Like sand through the nip of a waisted glass, salt
pools on a dark plate and waits – the old conceit –
for you to make your mark: tine-lines, knife-edge
asterisks, the swirls the tip of your finger chooses.

Like a father's test – *How much*? a daughter's sure reply –
Like fresh meat needs salt, love's necessary as air, as
oxygen to a blue flame, as a vital pinch to keep you
safe from the wrath of devils you don't believe in.

But here's un-holy salt on a plate, tap it back to flat,
to freshly fallen, clean-sheet white, imagine its sting
on the tip of your tongue, dip your finger in and wait.

Now make your mark, insignificant rune, that easy
hieroglyph, sweet conceit, that love will understand.

Glass

Too late to cross your fingers now, there's
blood, a splinter of glass under the skin
and seven years of it, if you believe it.

You believe it, too, like magpies and the pull
of a full moon, or a new moon seen through
glass: you turn the silver in your pocket, wish.

And now, first day of a new month and you say
the usual words – too late to stop yourself,
there's breath on them before you know it.

Under your skin you feel the splinter, watch
the blood dry over it; wait for the lightning.

The Rules of Frisbee

Let it be sunny, a Wednesday,
February, two hours after noon
when the frost has gone wet,
steamed off to a mirage of heat-haze.

Sit at a desk, in a row, in a room
(face the window), a room full of
heads down and listen. Hear the
scritching of pens, the shush-

shushing of graphite, watch
the sprint across A4 of ballpoint
and rollerball. Put down your pen,
tilt back your chair, jaunty,

clasp your hands at the back
of your head, elbows akimbo
and daydream, drift with the scene
in the frame of the window,

the open-air ballet of thrower to
catcher, catcher to thrower, leaping
like stars at the skim of the light-
hearted discus. Let it be sunny.

The Sisterhood

We are the canny measurers, controllers of the scales,
we set the tables, clear them, wash and wipe up,
dutiful as the shadows sewn to our heels.

A drop of vinegar to seal a cracked egg at a rolling boil,
a sprinkle of flour to cure a curdled creaming,
a metal spoon to cut & fold, to keep in air; we know

the energy it takes to whisk whites to the soft-peak stage,
the pinch of salt that's a trick of our mothers' trade
picked up at elbow, learned at marble slab, by syrup tin.

Thinner, paler than our mothers, we won't age like them
but shrink like sponges, grow down on our faces as we make
each day an empty bowl, a grain of rice saved up for,

a purple fruit to hold in the mouth before we bite, release
the stain, discover safe flesh and the hard of a stone to keep,
high and husbanded, against our puckered cheeks.

Stone, Scissors, Paper

i Stone:

>   Words stick in my mouth
>   like crusts that want soup: water,
>   salt, meat, a stir with a long spoon
>   and stones to trick an ungenerous host;
>   stones that rattle the pan at a rolling boil,
>   to scoop up, blow on, angling the steam
>   like a god; to be held in the mouth,
>   hard on the tongue, solid as words.

ii Scissors:

>   I have my own blades to grind:
>   when they fall I let them lie a while,
>   then warm them next to my heart
>   before I work them keen again
>   on the steady, turning stone.

iii Paper:

>   I've made it into boats, tigers,
>   fortune-pinchers, castles, turreted
>   and crisp with folding. I've burst
>   the quiet with it to anger gods, to eke
>   the long days into longer nights.
>   I've papered the walls of my house,
>   its slopes and angles, with the words
>   of strangers, lovers' messages, with signs.

Needlework

I come from a line of clever-fingered women, proud
make-do-and-menders, mistresses of sides-to-middle,
blanket-stitchers of raw edges, whose needles,
thread by thread, would pick up cloth worn thin
and weave it back to *good as new, invisible.*

Their ways are in me, blood, bone, muscle, viscera:
I am not one to weep at broken things, as when
a cup slips from a hand, tips, spills, scalds, shatters.
I know such things, like broken hearts, are everyday;
but when my needle finger aches for the snug of

a thimble, when I long for easy time to slip in like a cat
and curl up warm against me, I improvise, make do with
tambourines and paperchains, with cut hair, poems, fires.

The Rules of Fire

That sticks will be laid in a clinkered grate,
that yesterday's paper, twisted and screwed
will be tepee-d with kindling, balanced
by short-nailed fingers that know what they're at.

That Bryant & May will be shaken, slid open,
chosen, struck sulphurous. That Coalite will
smoke, glow, flicker, gutter and centrefold
sheets will be stretched till they scorch, until

furrows of soot are crept over with glow worms,
till hearth tiles crack and the chimney-draught
roars and flares livid.
                        That somewhere a siren will
let fly a torrent of holler and dog yelp, roller-skate,
bicycle, scooter & sandal, ear-splitting heart-thump,
stitch-in-the-ribs of the street-chase to be there,
to touch red, to see it set off.

The Bird

Right now it is out of its bell jar and breathing,
warm as before it was fashioned, stiffened,
remade as an artefact. Cock-eyed, sharp
as a parakeet, dark as a crow it is bristling
its plumage: a wet thing dragged out of the sea.

Sea, shoreline, swoop of the hills, forests
and rooftops – this is the map of its dreams
where it's drifted, circled, hovered, dropped
on its quarry; through unshifting years it has
held to the memory of unfolded wings, of flight,
kept faith to the vanishing moment of owning it all.

Now this: four flock-covered walls, velvet drapes
the colour of blood, weatherless air, the shiver
and pulse of its old heart restarting, sinew
and wing-muscle gathering power at the sight
of the sky, homeland of wind-lift, clear
as the dream and as still, still behind glass.

The Taxidermist

Most times it's knowing when to stop, to leave it,
to let go's the hardest bit; but this time something
ticks inside his chest. A small flip-flutter
and he's laying down his grooming brush,
standing back to look at hide and flank, at legs
as delicate as wishbones, those tricky, dainty hooves.

Glossed eyes like alleys shine at him, he knows
their fringes, lash by lash positioned by his steady hand
and sees that it is good, is finished. He folds his arms
across his chest and leans the weight of all his weariness
down through his heels, relieves the slow ache in his back
and sees that this is something other than his making, this

swell and symmetry of belly stripes that shift, as if a breath
is being taken, as if, somewhere inside, a heart is ticking.

Breathing

It begins at birth: an intake, then the awful quiet
while the virgin lung holds on, holds before
the first escape, the out-cry with its loss of breath.

Quick as that, breath kick-starts marvels –
the copycat tip of the tongue between the lips,
the clever mirroring of gesture; and eyes that
focus, follow, appear to recognise, to love.

We see ourselves reflected, carried on, don't see
the loss in growing, each breath counted out, each
cell displaced, replaced and somehow lessened.

Age thickens us with air that's heavy, toxic
with the teem and yowl of industry, until we
lose ourselves, till breathing is a letting go,
an easing, a disappearing echo in the dark.

Last Words

"Don't keep me, let me go"
—Charlotte Mew

She tamps and rolls with skilled fingers,
clever thumbs, she follows the paper's edge
with her tongue, lays down each slender
cigarette to a rough-cut row of smokes.

Tomorrow they'll burn slow, these tight-
packed mottled skins, they'll glow at each
pull of her lips, each drag of breath the thrill
of words burning, becoming caterpillars

of long ash, balanced for a moment, then
tapped to drop in a shower of shed skin.

Two Rivers Press has been publishing in and about Reading since 1994. Founded by the artist Peter Hay (1951–2003), the press continues to delight readers, local and further afield, with its varied list of individually designed, thought-provoking books.